THE HIDDEN SECRET TO WEALTH WITH CASH VALUE LIFE INSURANCE

Learn the Various Types of Life Insurance and How Life Insurance Can Serve as a Retirement Vehicle

Shane Collins

Table of Contents

AN INTRODUCTION TO CASH VALUE LIFE INSURANCE . 1

WHAT IS CASH VALUE INSURANCE VERSUS TERM LIFE INSURANCE? 6

WHAT TYPES OF PERMANENT LIFE INSURANCE HAVE CASH VALUE? 9

HOW CAN MY CASH VALUE LIFE INSURANCE MAKE ME MONEY? 21

THE BOTTOM LINE…IS CASH VALUE LIFE INSURANCE RIGHT FOR YOU? 39

MY PERSONAL EXPERIENCE 42

AN INTRODUCTION TO CASH VALUE LIFE INSURANCE

There are numerous ways to invest wisely to earn money and attain tax-free monetary growth. But, one method many individuals don't know about is using cash value life insurance policies to do just this – earn money and attain tax-free growth while investing income wisely.

Everyone knows that life insurance is a way to protect your loved ones financially if you die. But, many people don't realize that cash value life insurance acts as an investment, with a savings component built into your life insurance. This cash component gains value, tax-deferred with interest, as the years go by and can be borrowed against or used as collateral, similar to a loan, when you need some extra cash.

How does this work? Cash value life insurance policies provide monetary coverage while you are living, as well as a death benefit that will go to your loved ones after you die. Each month you pay your premiums similar to term life insurance. However, with a cash value life insurance policy, a portion of your premiums are paid into an investment-type account (i.e., the cash value), while the remainder goes towards death benefits for your beneficiaries. The portion that goes into the investment-type account grows through accruing interest over time (depending on which type of cash value life insurance plan you choose). This cash value is essentially "liquid" and can become a valuable source of income when times are tough or in the case of an emergency.

Although extra cash in your pocket sounds tempting, there is a lot to think about when choosing a cash value insurance policy over the standard term life insurance. First, there are different forms of cash value life insurance from which to choose. Second, cash value life insurance usually has a lower rate of return compared to investing in stocks. Third, cash value life insurance has higher premiums, higher fees from the insurance company, and higher commissions from agents.

That being said, cash value insurance policies are not just for the rich and America's "elite" one percent. If researched, chosen, and used correctly, a cash value life insurance plan can become a lucrative savings account that can be used to withdraw funds, attain a loan, or even pay off your very own insurance premiums. All of these benefits are available with cash value life insurance, in addition to growing a death benefit that will protect your loved ones after you die. Isn't that the whole point of life insurance? To protect your beneficiaries after you die?

Yes, the main function of life insurance is to ensure your family's financial well-being after you are no longer there to provide for them financially. Just think of all the bills you pay every day – mortgage, food, entertainment, college education...the list can go on and on. If you aren't there to pay these bills, your life insurance plan is there to replace your income. But, what if you could also benefit from your life insurance plan while you were living? That is what cash value life insurance offers you.

You can withdraw funds or take out a loan in case of an emergency; you can build another nest egg to be used towards your retirement; you can pay off your premiums with the cash invested instead of paying them out of pocket. You can even boost the death benefit for your loved ones with this extra cash. All in all, a cash value life insurance plan allows you to use these funds while you are living, while also protecting those you love after you die. And, all of this is done tax free!

This article will discuss the following in detail:
1. Cash value life insurance (also called permanent life insurance) versus term life insurance.
2. The different types of cash value life insurance:
    a. Whole life insurance;
    b. Variable life insurance;
    c. universal life insurance, and
    d. indexed universal life insurance.
1. How cash value life insurance makes money.
2. How you can get and use your cash:

a. Withdraw funds;
b. Take out a loan;
c. Pay off your premiums;
d. Boost your death benefit;
e. Build your retirement;
f. Surrender the life insurance policy;
g. Sell your life insurance to a third party.

Most people think life insurance is only a way to make provisions and protect your loved ones after your death. But, what if you could invest in life insurance that also builds a cash value to be used at a later date while you're still alive? That's exactly the benefit of cash value life insurance. A cash value life insurance plan will protect your loved ones after you die through a death benefit that pays out when the policyholder dies, but will also serve as a liquid financial savings account while you're living. This is because your premiums are split between the death benefit and a cash value (along with any fees and overheads the insurance company charges to provide the coverage). This cash value operates as a tax-sheltered investment plan and earns interest on your premium payments. You can use these earnings while you are alive to withdraw as cash, attain a loan, or even pay your monthly premiums.

IMPORTANT NOTE: Because the cash value portion of your life insurance policy is separate from your death benefit, your beneficiaries would not receive this cash benefit if you die before it is used. That is, they will receive the death benefit promised, but not the cash value earnings in the investment portion of the policy. Instead, this cash portion is returned to the insurance company since it is basically the liquid amount you would have received if you would have cancelled your coverage. So, you need to make sure you use this money while you are alive so the cash value isn't surrendered to your insurance policy if you pass away!

WHAT IS CASH VALUE INSURANCE VERSUS TERM LIFE INSURANCE?

Term life insurance is the other option one can choose to protect their loved ones. If you choose term life insurance, you are basically insuring yourself for a specific number of years and, if you die during those chosen years, the insurance company pays your loved ones. However, if you outlive the term, the policy simply ends and you don't receive any cash. On the other hand, cash value life insurance does have a death benefit for your loved ones similar to term life insurance, but also gives you cash-on-hand while you are living.

As long as you, the policyholder, make your regular premium payments to keep your policy active, your beneficiaries will receive what's called a "death benefit" – an agreed-upon amount of money – after you die. But, cash value life insurance also has an investment element that can earn interest, build over time, and be available for withdrawal at a later date. Essentially, cash value is a "living" benefit of life insurance; the monies don't sit stagnant only to be used after you die. Instead, you can take cash out when you are living in lieu of waiting until after your death, in which case the cash goes to your beneficiaries.

How does this work? Your premium payments are split between funding the death benefit portion and funding the cash value of your plan. Over time, the cash value component – essentially, your savings or investment component – grows while the death benefit shrinks. In addition, if you, the policy holder, die after the cash value of the policy is fully realized, the entire amount paid to your beneficiaries ultimately comes from the cash value side, not the death benefit side.

Cash value life insurance is a form of permanent life insurance; that is, it is a policy that provides lifetime coverage and flexibility to cancel your policy, attain the cash value of your policy, or withdraw monies for emergencies. While term life insurance guarantees a death benefit to your beneficiaries at a specific time – your death – permanent life insurance provides coverage and cash value while you are living. As long as the premiums are paid, cash value life insurance provides coverage for your entire life. Term life insurance does not include a cash value, which is why they are usually more affordable than permanent life insurance options.

Cash value life insurance policies usually have higher premiums that term life insurance due to the added lifetime flexibility. That being said, a cash value policy earns interest and defers taxes on these accumulated earnings. The only circumstance in which you could get cash back from a term life insurance policy is if you have a return of premium rider – an add-on policy that returns the premiums you have paid if you outlive the term of the policy. Otherwise, if you decide to just have term life insurance coverage with the insurer, you will not receive anything in return because term life insurance policies do not have a cash value.

So, while your term life insurance provides temporary coverage over a certain period of time – 10, 20, 30, 50 years – it provides no additional cash value. You cannot borrow against a term life policy or cash it in for money if you need it. This is what makes term life insurance so much more affordable since the premiums are usually lower than permanent life insurance. Although cash value life insurance is pricier, it offers an additional savings component.

Another benefit of cash value life insurance is the stability of the insurance itself. You are going to be insured under the plan in spite of how your health may change over time. If your health begins to decline and you have term life insurance, you may need to purchase another term (also called "re-upping" your coverage), which may come with higher premiums when you are at your most vulnerable. This is not the case with cash value life insurance; with this type of policy, you are covered even if your health changes over time. Although you are paying higher premiums with this plan, these premiums remain a flat rate no matter what health issues you may encounter as you get older.

As the policyholder of a cash value policy, you are able to use the cash value of your policy for numerous purposes, whether you need a loan to be paid back at a later date, cash on hand, or even money to help pay your premiums. How does this work?

WHAT TYPES OF PERMANENT LIFE INSURANCE HAVE CASH VALUE?

The way the cash value portion of your life insurance policy works depends on the type of policy you have, and there are four types of permanent life insurance policies that have a cash value: whole life, variable life, universal life, and indexed universal life insurance. Deciding which type of permanent life insurance to choose ultimately depends on how much risk you are willing to take with your cash.

Whole Life Insurance – This is the most common type of permanent life insurance because it's the most straightforward. This type of insurance guarantees a fixed rate of return on your cash value. The annual price you pay, the death benefit your beneficiaries receive, and the return you attain on the cash value component are all clear, uncomplicated, and upfront.

Whole life offers a savings component for the duration of your entire life and allows you to build your cash value at a fixed rate (determined by the insurer). This type of insurance is designed to reach the size of the death benefit when the policy matures. As for the death benefit, as long as your premiums are paid, while life insurance will provide your loved ones a death benefit after you die.

This is what makes whole life insurance such an attractive form of permanent life insurance – it offers a death benefit while still allowing you to build a cash value you can borrow against. A guaranteed death benefit plus a guaranteed cash value makes for a very attractive permanent life insurance plan.

Through your whole life insurance plan, your cash grows by earning interest at a rate pre-determined by the insurer, and your premiums remain level over the course of your life. This type of cash value insurance plan is definitely the least risky compared to other permanent life insurance options because whole life insurance offers a guaranteed cash value. Essentially, it operates similar to a standard savings account; the policy earns interest at a predetermined rate.

Whole life insurance makes it easy to take advantage of the cash value portion of your policy. This cash value builds over time and the policy holder can make withdraws, as needed, or borrow against the monies that act as a savings component within the policy itself. The cash value within whole life insurance earns a guaranteed minimum amount of interest and can serve as a solid investment plan.

Although you cannot deduct your whole life insurance premiums on your tax return, there are many tax-free benefits that will be discussed below. In addition, when your beneficiaries receive the death benefit portion of this policy, they will not have to pay federal taxes on this death benefit amount. All in all, the risk on whole life insurance is low: you will have a predictable rate of return, fixed premiums, and guaranteed death benefit for your loved ones.

NOTE: You cannot increase your living and death benefits under whole life insurance unless you add a paid-up policy. This option is not available with all whole life insurance plans, so you will need to contact your specific insurance provider to see if this option is available. If it is, paid-up additions is essentially additional insurance that allows the policy holder to increase their living and death benefits by increasing the cash value. This could be a valuable option if you have a very large cash value in your plan but you do not need to use it on yourself while you are living. Instead, it can be used to make sure your family does not lose this additional cash value that you have built up over the years.

Paid-up additions also allow you to pay premiums using the policy's cash value due to this conversion because the cash value ends up being substantial enough to allow you to stop paying premiums out-of-pocket. The cash value of paid-up additional insurance increases over time, which is tax-deferred. Basically, a paid-up addition gives a higher guaranteed net cash value sooner than a basic whole life insurance plan. Paid-up additions earn dividends, which compound over time. However, each premium payment, if paid with the cash value, is also deducted from the policy's death benefit.

Buying paid-up additions does not require more medical exams or underwriting, although it is very similar to buying a smaller, single-premium life insurance policy. So, if your health has gotten worse over time, you can still look into purchasing paid-up additions as an added benefit to your plan.

Variable life insurance – This type of insurance also covers you for the duration of your life and has a guaranteed death benefit. However, variable life insurance does not hold the guaranteed cash value seen with whole life insurance. Instead, your money is invested in various "sub-accounts," which are a pool of in-house investor funds offered by the insurer. This is how your cash grows (or shrinks) over time.

With this type of plan, your cash value will grow similar to a traditional investment plan; that is, it grows at the interest rate of a predetermined index specifically chosen by the life insurance company. Your cash value is invested in specifically-chosen aggregated portfolios, similar to mutual funds, but this means your cash is less insulated from market fluctuations. While whole life insurance works similar to a standard savings account, variable life insurance works similar to a standard investment account. Although the premiums for this plan are also fixed, some variable life insurance accounts may offer "adjustable" premiums, which allow you to change, modify, or adjust your premium and death benefit options as you continue to invest the cash value into the sub-accounts offered by the life insurance company.

This type of plan holds more risk than the standard whole life insurance option, including the risk of possessing a more expensive insurance plan that could end up with little or no cash value depending on the market, because your cash growth is tied to a stock index (such as the Standard & Poor's 500). So, you could either gain the greatest returns on your money if your stocks, bonds or mutual funds do well, or you could lose your cash value if your investments tank. Is there reward with this investment risk? Yes…variable life insurance gives you the opportunity to invest in sub-accounts that may offer higher rates of return.

That being said, this type of plan has additional rewards that can outweigh any investment risk. For example with a variable life insurance plan your premiums are adjustable. What does that mean? You have the option to skip a premium payment or even stop paying your premiums all together if the cash value of your policy can cover those costs (similar to universal life insurance, discussed below). This option is very helpful if you have an emergency and need to skip a premium payment or two during those more difficult months. In addition, if you transfer funds between investments, you can do this tax-free, in addition to your ability to withdraw funds or take a loan out against the cash value when times are tough. Just make note of what these withdraws may do to your death benefit. Finally, if your insurance needs change as you age, you can either increase or decrease your coverage under this plan, whether it is on your death benefit or on the policy's cash value.

Flexibility is key to this permanent insurance plan. If you enjoy reviewing different investment options and can take the time to better understand where you should invest your funds, variable life insurance allows for these flexible possibilities. The main aspect to understand is, like any other type of investment option, there is always the possibility of loss when playing the market, which would reduce your policy's cash value.

Universal life insurance – Another option that covers you for the duration of your life and offers a guaranteed life benefit is universal life insurance. This type of policy is less risky than variable life insurance since the guaranteed cash value is protected from investment risk since the cash grows at a fixed interest rate. However, these monies could also be depleted to pay for premiums. In addition, these premiums are not level; instead, they vary and are subject to federal tax laws.

How does universal life insurance work? Similar to the other options, when you pay your premiums each month a portion of each payment builds up your cash value while the other portion goes towards the death benefit. However, a universal life insurance policy also offers flexibility with premiums; this type of insurance has the option to adjust your premiums and death benefit, similar to the variable life insurance option. If you hold a universal life insurance policy, you have the option to either lower your premiums or even stop paying them as long as the cash value of your policy can cover the monthly costs. This is a very advantageous option when times are tough. You just always need to make sure your cash value can cover your premium costs.

Along with this benefit, you will continue to earn a cash value through interest, and you can withdraw money or take out a loan against it similar to whole and variable life insurance. As long as you take note that the amount you withdraw or borrow many reduce the policy's death benefit in certain cases, similar to variable life insurance, this option is a good mixture of the benefits of both whole and variable life insurance.

How is the risk with this plan different from whole and variable life insurance? The cash value portion of a universal life insurance policy earns interest similar to the current money market rates. Although this means the interest earned may go down if the market goes down, some universal plans do offer a minimum performance guarantee with these types of policies.

Although universal and variable life insurance are very similar, there are significant differences between universal life insurance and whole life insurance that must be understood in order to make the best decision of permanent life insurance. Both offer lifelong protection and a cash value as long as premiums are paid, but:

1. Adjustable versus fixed premiums – Universal life insurance policies allow for the ability to adjust your premium amounts, while whole life insurance only offers fixed premiums and death benefits.
2. Adjustable versus fixed death benefit – Similar to the premiums, universal life insurance policies also allow for the

ability to adjust your death benefit amount, while this benefit remains fixed if using the whole life insurance option.

3. Interest on cash value differences – Universal life insurance interest is in line with the current money market rates, which could mean hefty rewards or unfortunate losses. Whole life insurance offers a guaranteed rate of return, which lowers the risk when earning interest. However, this also does not allow for the benefit of higher interest earnings when the market is doing well.

In short, universal life insurance plans allow you to vary your premiums and your death benefit coverage amount. They also offer varying levels of risk depending on the market – there is a strong potential for gains for your cash value if you choose a universal life insurance plan.

Indexed Universal Life Insurance – This final option gives a cash value benefit based upon the performance of a market index like the S&P 500. Therefore, the funds do not earn a fixed rate of interest similar to whole life insurance but, since the monies are not directly invested into the stock market, there is less risk with this plan. So, this is another potential option to build cash value over the long term. How does this work?

Your insurer will choose the index, calculate an interest based on the chosen index's performance, and then credits the interest to your cash value account. However, you do not lose everything if the market crashes since indexed universal life insurance guarantees a minimum interest rate to be paid even if the index produces lower returns.

That being said, this plan is also subject to a cap on the upper interest limit even if the market goes through the roof.

There are other similarities between this type of plan and the others discussed:

1. Adjustable premium payments (within certain limits) and the ability to use your cash value to pay your premiums.
2. Adjustable death benefit, which can be lowered at any time (increasing them is more complicated and may require a new medical examination).
3. The ability to withdraw funds from the cash value portion of the policy or borrow against it (subject to interest charges). These monies can be accessed at any time, regardless of your age. However, this may reduce your death benefit or cause your policy to lapse if you do not maintain a certain balance within the cash value portion of the account.
4. Tax-deferred cash accrual while preserving a death benefit for loved ones.

In the end, indexed universal life insurance is a good mixture of all three forms of permanent life insurances discussed above. It offers the potential of interest growth based on how the market performs, but also guarantees a certain amount of protection from losing all of its value if the market tanks.

Remember…while whole life insurance guarantees a fixed rate interest model that may not have a huge potential growth factor, variable life insurance grows with the market, which could offer potential highs as well as potential lows. Universal life is a good mixture of the two in that it offers fixed-rate and variable rate models to invest in if you wish. Indexed universal life is a good option if you want to allocate your cash value amounts to either a fixed or equity index account based on popular indexes like the S&P 500. These policies may be more unpredictable than universal life insurance. However, they are less risky than variable universal life policies and still may see larger growth than whole life insurance.

In the end…indexed universal life insurance may be a great option for those who desire a cash value that can grow through a solid equity index along with the protection of permanent life insurance through a guaranteed death benefit. Its flexibility and safety all wrapped up into one!

Basically, the total amount of your cash value is credited, with interest based on any increases in an equity index. Because there is less risk than variable policies, this form of permanent insurance guarantees a minimum fixed interest rate along with a varied choice of indexes in which to choose. In addition, you can also decide what percentage you would like allocated to the fixed and indexed portions of your accounts! Basically, the value of your selected index is documented at the beginning of the month and then compared to the value at the end of the month. If you see an increase in your index, this interest is added to your cash value. That is, your index gains are credited back to your policy.

For example:

If you see a 7% increase from the beginning of September to the end of September, this 7% is then multiplied by your cash value and the subsequent interest is then added to that cash value. Now, if the index goes down, then no interest is credited to the cash account. But, you are still protected in this plan from losing everything! Basically, your goal is to outperform the chosen market index.

This, however, could also be seen as a con since the insurance company has the ability to cap your highs and lows. But, this option is also attractive because, since there is some risk, the premiums will more than likely be lower than the whole life insurance option. In addition, your cash value can pay your insurance premiums if you build enough equity, allowing you to all but stop making out-of-pocket payments.

If you would like the security of a fixed universal life policy or whole insurance and the interest-earning potential of a variable policy, indexed universal life is a great option!

Remember…

Depending on which type of cash value life insurance policy you choose will determine what dividends you earn from your payments each month. Dividends are not guaranteed for each and every cash value life insurance policy, but when they are distributed they are according to the type of policy you have and the amount of your cash value. In addition, you may have an insurance company that pays you what's called an "annual dividend." This is usually money that is left over from the premiums you paid that year after the insurance company's expenses and claims are paid. These are also nontaxable since the IRS deems them as a return of your premium, not a traditional dividend. You can use these dividends for a variety of things, from withdrawing them as cash, to buying additional coverage, to beefing up your death benefit, or even paying your monthly premiums.

HOW CAN MY CASH VALUE LIFE INSURANCE MAKE ME MONEY?

s discussed above, cash value life insurance is a form of permanent life insurance that offers two features:

1. A death benefit – the amount of money that is paid out to your beneficiaries when you die.
2. Cash value – an investment-like feature that accrues cash to be used in a variety of ways while you are alive.

Each month, a portion of your premiums are paid into the investment portion of your policy, while the remainder goes into the death benefit for your loved ones protection. The benefits? Tax-free earnings and cash on hand for a variety of options, from withdrawals and loans to paying premiums and saving for retirement:

Tax-free earnings: Probably the best advantage of cash value life insurance is the tax advantage. Similar to other investment options, the cash value of your life insurance policy and the earnings it accrues are tax-free. You can continue to keep these funds tax-free as long as you only withdraw an amount that does not go over what you have paid in premiums. Therefore, it is recommended to not withdraw more than this amount, as you will have to pay taxes on the difference between what you have already paid in premiums and the amount of cash you are taking out of your policy. The basic rule of thumb is to only make a tax-free withdraw up to the amount you have already paid into the cash-value portion of your insurance policy. If your withdraw exceeds that amount, it will then become taxable income.

Cash on hand: The reason individuals decide to purchase permanent life insurance is because of the cash value. This is the main benefit of cash value life insurance – you have cash on hand if needed while you are living. This is because the cash value element of your policy is basically an investment plan. Therefore, you can do many things with this cash that is similar to a traditional investment tool. The important thing to note, however, is the cash portion of your permanent life insurance plan is a "use it or lose it" scenario. This cash will not be available to your beneficiaries after you die unless you allocate it to the death benefit portion of your plan before your passing.

FOR EXAMPLE: Let's say you hold a policy that has a $50,000 death benefit and you have accumulated $5,000 in cash value. Upon your death, your insurance will pay the full death benefit of $50,000 to your beneficiaries. However, the $5,000 you saved in the cash value portion of your policy will ultimately go back to the insurance provider. So technically, the real liability cost to the insurance company is $45,000 since they retain your $5,000 in cash. After you die, your beneficiaries receive the death benefit, but any remaining cash value will be returned to the insurance company. So, you will need to spend this cash value while you are living!

There are seven ways you can use this cash so that you ensure this money remains yours and not the insurance company's:

1. You can simply withdraw the funds, but if the money is not repaid these withdraws will reduce the policy's death benefit;
2. You can take out a loan by borrowing against your cash value, but will need to repay it, with interest, to preserve the death benefit portion of the policy;
3. You can use the cash (in some cases) to pay off your premiums once the cash value reaches a certain level;
4. You can use the cash to increase the death benefit left to your loved ones after you die;
5. You can supplement another form of retirement savings, such as a 401k or IRA;
6. You can surrender the policy and withdraw all of the cash value in the policy if you no longer need life insurance. However, you should note that if you decide to surrender your coverage to the insurer and cash out early, there will be fees charged that will take away from the policy's cash value; and,
7. You could sell your life insurance policy to a third party for a cash settlement.

1. Withdraw your funds: At any point during your life, you can withdraw cash from your permanent life insurance policy up to your policy's basis (i.e., the amount you have paid into the policy for your premiums). Basically, with cash value life insurance, the portion of the payments you make towards your premiums build the cash value portion of the account and forms your policy's basis. This is essentially your money – your savings so to speak – so you are free to withdraw your own cash for emergencies, vacations, payment of bills, to help fund retirement, whatever you like. Maybe you are low on funds one month or have a large purchase you would like to make and do not have the cash on hand. As long as you do not exceed this basis, these withdrawals will not be taxed. However, if you withdraw more than your basis, these monies will be taxed at your current income tax rate.

You will need to find out if your specific policy allows for unlimited withdrawals or a finite amount each calendar year, as each permanent life insurance plan is different. Also remember that your withdrawal is only tax-free if it does not exceed the amount you have already paid into the cash value portion of your policy. This is very important to be aware of, as you do not want to end up paying taxes on your withdrawals.

NOTE: Although withdrawing funds gives you access to cash that can be used for anything you need, it is important to note that your death benefit will also be reduced based on the amount you withdraw, so make sure your timing is right (that is, your beneficiaries will not need the full death benefit amount at that time!). That being said, if your beneficiaries are adult children, for example, who are financially stable and may not need a larger inheritance, you may want to withdraw a portion of your cash value for your own needs and still pass on a smaller inheritance. Just be aware that your cash withdrawals can take a financial toll on your death benefit or even wipe the entire amount out without you realizing it until it is too late.

These "partial withdrawals" are handled differently depending on what type of permanent life insurance plan you choose. For example, experts do not recommend making partial withdrawals if you have a whole life insurance policy because the death benefit may be reduced at a greater amount than your withdrawal. That is, the death benefit for your beneficiaries ends up being reduced by a greater amount than what you actually withdrew in cash. However, making a partial withdrawal using variable and universal life insurance policies, which have the investment option, are usually less complicated. As noted above, as long as you do not withdraw more than your policy's basis – the amount you have paid for your premiums – you can make partial withdrawals tax free and they only reduce the death benefit payment by the exact amount you withdraw.

2. Take out a loan: Another option for accessing the cash portion of your permanent life insurance policy is taking out a loan from the cash value portion of your insurance plan. Taking out a loan is a very common way to access funds from a cash value life insurance policy. This process is different from making a standard withdraw because you are basically borrowing *against* your policy. Normally, you have the

ability to borrow the amount up to the cash value of your insurance policy. Because your premium payments are split each month between the cash value and death benefit, the amount you borrow can also include the portion of your paid premiums that have gone towards the cash value portion of your account and any accrued interest on those monies. Therefore, you can borrow from your cash value account, tax free, if you need a loan with low interest rates that does not have a specific date by which it needs to be paid back.

This option acts like any other traditional loan; you make an agreement on the amount you would like loaned to you and the insurance issuer will charge interest on the outstanding principal of the loan. This interest is an additional charge, usually lower than most standard interest rates, so it will need to be paid out-of-pocket or, if available, from the cash value portion of the insurance plan. If you do not pay the interest annually, it will simply be added to the amount of the loan needed to be paid back. However, interest will continue to accrue, so manage your loan wisely. Remember, life insurance companies are like any other business – their main goal is to make money. And, since they cannot make money off of you if you take your money out of your plan (yes, the insurance company, like a standard bank, will use your money that is sitting in your plan to cover overheads, invest, and pay other people's claims) they will instead charge you interest to make up those differences. Although you can keep the loan as long as you would like, note that you will continuously accrue interest on those funds.

However, you do not need a credit check like traditional loans, so a loan from your cash value life insurance will not appear on your credit report like other loans would. In addition, there are not any underwriting requirements since the insurer basically holds the funds to cover the loan already and there is no time limit on the loan – you can keep it as long as you need.

The process for applying for this type of loan is also much easier than a standard loan from a bank. These monies can be used for anything, from improving your home, to buying a car, to paying off financial obligations.

Similar to withdrawing cash outright, your outstanding loan amount also reduces the death benefit. If the interest on the loan remains unpaid, the insurance company may deduct that amount from the cash value that remains in the permanent life insurance policy.

NOTE: Although there is no time limit on how long you can keep your loan, if you die before your loan is paid off, the remaining amount owed will be subtracted from the death benefit your beneficiaries will receive from the policy. For example, if you take out a loan and then are in a plane crash (morbid, but it happens), and the loan is more than the death benefit, your family will not receive a penny from your cash value life insurance policy. Instead, the death benefit will be used to pay off your loan. This is simply because the loan is connected to your death benefit as well as the cash value portion of your insurance policy plan. Therefore, before you decide to take a loan out against your cash value life insurance policy, ask yourself one question: *if I day the day after I take out a loan against my life insurance, will there still be enough money in the death benefit portion of the plan to take care of my family? Isn't this the reason you took out life insurance in the first place? To take care of your loved ones in the event of your passing?*

So, the question remains, when is a suitable time to borrow against your cash value life insurance policy? If you need a loan but a conventional loan from your bank is not an option, either because of high interest rates or a low credit score, then taking out a loan against your permanent life insurance policy is a great option. If you have the opportunity to get a conventional loan from your bank, however, with a lower interest rate, this is often the better choice in the long run for both you and your beneficiaries.

In addition, don't forget that, like any other loan, the loan you take out against your permanent insurance policy accrues interest. This accruing amount could also chip away at your policy's death benefit since the loan amount, plus interest, is deducted from the death benefit allocated to your beneficiaries if you die and these amounts are paid off. So, think wisely before taking out a loan against your cash value life insurance policy. Although the low interest rates are attractive, adding a loan, plus interest, to your financial obligations may not be wise due to the negative effects it could have on your death benefit. In addition, most loans must have income taxes paid on the amounts, and if the size of your loan exceeds the value of your policy (possibly because of unpaid interest) your policy will lapse and your coverage will be dropped. This is why you need to monitor the loan, especially because there is no deadline on which it needs to be paid back. The interest on the cash you borrow for your loan will accrue continuously and possibly chip away at the death benefit portion allocated for your loved ones.

In the end, borrowing against your cash value life insurance could be an advantageous financial choice, but ultimately depends on one's current financial and health situation. What are your current financial and health circumstances? What plans do you have for this loan and ultimately paying it back, plus interest? You need to weigh the advantages and disadvantages to borrowing against your cash value, as well as your current life situations and circumstances, also compare this to taking out a loan with your bank.

Finally, taking out a loan is ultimately dependent on how much cash value you have in your account. Remember that whole and universal life insurance policies, although very low risk, take time to build and may not be liquid enough to borrow against right away. That being said, if you have accumulated a generous cash value within your life insurance policy, then choosing to take out a loan could be very beneficial financially. Borrowing against your cash value is the perfect choice if your insurance policy has a very high cash value or if you are looking to "re-invest" these funds at a higher rate of return than the interest you are accruing on the loan itself. The interest will be lower than your traditional bank loan and you are not obligated to pay it back in a specified amount of time. As long as you are aware that you must pay back the loan ,as well as the interest before you die, you may want to take out a loan from your permanent life insurance policy versus taking out a loan from your traditional bank.

In the end, just remember that the whole point of life insurance, even a cash value life insurance plan, is to provide financial stability to your loved ones after you pass away. If you borrow too much against your policy, you risk not having anything left for your beneficiaries if you die unexpectedly. That being said, you can use your loan for anything – even to pay your premiums and keep your insurance stable if times are tough financially. Or, you can even pay off your premiums using the cash value portion of your permanent life insurance policy.

3. Pay your policy premiums: Once you have accumulated a sufficient amount of cash value, variable and universal life insurance policies (and paid-up portions of whole life insurance policies) give you the opportunity to use your policy's cash value to pay your insurance premiums. Once the cash value portion of your life insurance policy reaches a certain amount where it can cover the payments, this cash value can also be used to pay your policy premiums in lieu of paying them out-of-pocket. This is a very advantageous feature of permanent life insurance policies versus term life insurance since permanent life insurance usually costs more than term.

With a term life insurance plan, the money you pay to cover your insurance premiums does not have any return on investment. The insurance company keeps these monies and you cannot claim these funds during your lifetime. However, with cash value life insurance, a portion of your payments goes into building the cash value of your policy. Therefore, these monies can be made available to pay your premiums when times are financially tough. As long as you have a sufficient amount in this cash value portion, you can stop paying your premiums out-of-pocket and, instead, have the cash value portion of your policy cover them.

This option of how to attain your cash can be very attractive – you are short on cash so you decide to stop paying your insurance premiums and, instead, earmark the cash value portion of your policy to cover them. But like anything else when it comes to using the cash value portion of your life insurance policy, there are aspects of which you must be aware.

First, you need to carefully monitor the cash value of your policy to make sure it does not drop too low. If you do not monitor how much cash is being used to pay for your premiums, you may end up depleting all of the cash in this portion of your life insurance policy. If you exhaust the cash value of your life insurance policy then your policy will lapse, which will terminate your life insurance coverage. Therefore, you need to make sure your cash value is not too small if you want to use it to pay off your insurance premiums. That being said, if you have a sizable amount of cash built up in your policy, and your variable or universal life insurance plans have consistent returns on investment, you can keep your life insurance and not pay premiums for years and years.

FOR EXAMPLE: If your variable or universal life insurance policy has an annual premium of $2,500 and you have $100,000 in cash value, you would only need to make 2.5% interest annually to pay off your premiums in their entirety using your cash value and not lose any money!

Since the cash value of whole life insurance policies usually grows at a slower (but less risky) rate, whole life insurance policies usually do not allow policy holders to use the cash to pay premiums unless a paid-up policy is purchased. As discussed earlier, paid-up additions to your whole life insurance plan acts like a smaller, additional insurance policy that can be used to increase the living and death benefits or to use the cash to pay off premiums. Adding this paid-up option is a valuable alternative if you have a very large cash value in your plan but you do not need to use it on yourself while you are living. Instead of withdrawing the funds or taking out a loan for yourself, you can simply use it to pay your annual premiums and never pay them out-of-pocket again.

Paid-up additions are an advantageous option for whole life insurance holders to pay premiums using the policy's cash value because the cash value ends up being substantial enough to allow you to stop paying premiums out-of-pocket. This paid-up addition gives a higher guaranteed net cash value sooner than a basic whole life insurance plan and earns dividends, which compound in value over time.

However, each premium payment, if paid with the cash value, is deducted from the policy's death benefit and could end up giving you less cash value available for other purposes, such as a policy withdrawal or loan.

Nearly all variable, universal, and "paid-up" whole life insurance policies allow policy holders to pay for life insurance premiums using the cash value portion of the policy, but some plans may have limitations. For example, some plans only allow you to use your accumulated cash to pay for premiums after you have had the policy for a minimum of one year. Other polices require enough cash value to subsidize the policy for a minimum of 60 days in order to complete the request. That being said, if you have enough cash to stop paying your premiums out-of-pocket, you could be saving yourself thousands of dollars in expenses each year.

4. Increase your death benefit: Maybe you have accumulated a generous cash value within your permanent life insurance policy over time and simply do not need to use the funds on yourself. If this is the case, it may be a great idea to use this cash to leave an even larger death benefit to your beneficiaries. But, how is this done?

Usually, transferring the funds from the cash portion of your permanent life insurance policy to the death benefit portion just takes a phone call; let your insurance company know you are interested in increasing the death benefit using the cash value portion of your policy. Just make sure your insurance company will honor this request without limitations.

If you have the means, you should try to deplete as much of your cash value as possible so that those monies go to your beneficiaries when you die, not the insurance company.

FOR EXAMPLE: If you have a variable life insurance policy with a $500,000 death benefit and $100,000 in cash value, and you know you do not need to spend that $100,000 on yourself, you should transfer the entire cash amount to increase the death benefit to $600,000. That way, the extra $100,000 in cash – which is *your* money – will go to your loved ones and not the life insurance company if you die unexpectedly.

5. Supplement your retirement savings: Nearly all of us have some form of retirement plan to live on once we are no longer working, whether it is a 401(k) from our current job or a traditional or Roth individual retirement account. However, if you have accumulated a hefty cash value in your permanent life insurance account, these funds can be used to strengthen your current retirement portfolio.

Whole life insurance, in particular, can be a very worthwhile complement to your retirement plan when you are ready to retire. Unlike term life insurance, which more than likely will run out when you are ready to retire, a whole life insurance policy will cover you until you die. In addition, the monies in whole life insurance grow tax-deferred, which can accumulate a hefty nest egg over time for your retirement years. However, if you find you do not need this policy when you are ready to retire, why not cash it out, save money on the monthly premiums, and use the cash value as retirement funds?

You can also use the cash value portion of your life insurance policy as a strategy to save money for retirement or supplement your retirement fund. For example, if the market has a bad year, which does not affect a whole life insurance policy but does affect your IRA, you can use the cash value portion of your policy instead of your retirement savings. That way, you can allow your IRA to replenish after a bad market year and, instead, make withdraws from your whole life insurance plan.

6. Surrender your permanent life insurance policy: If you find you no longer need your permanent life insurance policy, you can surrender it back to the insurance company and collect the cash value (minus any loans, unpaid premiums, and additional fees). Surrendering your permanent life insurance isn't complicated, as you simply tell your insurance agent you no longer want to carry your insurance coverage and they will begin the cash-out process. If you are curious as to how much net cash value you would receive from a surrender it is usually listed separately on your permanent life insurance statements as the "actual" surrender value of the policy. However, you should take many life, financial, and health factors into consideration before taking this irreversible route to accessing your cash.

Probably the most important consideration when contemplating a full surrender is the death benefit. If you surrender your permanent life insurance policy, you will also be surrendering the death benefit portion of your policy meant for your loved ones. What does this mean? Basically, your beneficiaries will no longer receive those funds when you die.

NOTE: The actual net cash value will be lower than the total value you have accumulated over the years because there will be additional fees assessed. Therefore, if you decide to surrender your permanent life insurance policy, this option will reduce the cash value you ultimately receive. So, you should hold on to your policy for a minimum of ten to 15 years to make sure the net cash value is closer to the total accumulated cash value you have built over time. That being said, you can technically surrender the value of your policy after a minimum three years of holding that policy and accumulating cash value. This may not be a smart move, however, in that the surrender fees could eat up the smaller cash value you accumulated over this shorter period of time. In addition, if you surrender the policy during what is known as the "surrender period," which is anywhere between the first two to three years of ownership, you may not receive any cash value or be subject to even more additional, larger fees. You should talk to your insurance agent about the potential surrender fees that could be assessed depending on how long you have owned your permanent life insurance policy.

You should also be aware that the cash you ultimately receive after you surrender your insurance will be subject to income tax. Any money you receive from the surrender that is over the "cash basis" (how much you originally paid into the policy) will be taxed accordingly.

Probably the most important thing to note, however, is if you surrender your life insurance you and your loved ones are no longer protected if you die. A surrender essentially means you are giving up your insurance policy. Now, you do receive the cash value, less any fees, and there is no interest or repayment like you would have if you took out a loan against the policy. But, surrendering your policy means you will no longer have life insurance, your beneficiaries will no longer have a death benefit, and because of this you should have an alternative plan in place for further protection against uncertainties.

If you decide to go down the route of surrendering your permanent life insurance policy, you should first talk to your life insurance agent or your financial adviser. You could also consider selling your life insurance plan to a third party.

7. Sell your permanent life insurance policy for a settlement: The final option for obtaining the cash value of your permanent life insurance policy is to opt for what's called a "life settlement. You are still giving up your life insurance policy, similar to an all-out surrender, but in this case you are selling your policy to a third party for essentially a cash sale. This could be a very advantageous option if the premiums for your policy are too high and unaffordable, your beneficiaries are financially secure on their own, or you no longer have beneficiaries to obtain your death benefit after you die.

If you are interested in going this route, the first question you will need to ask yourself is whether or not you can even sell your life insurance policy for a cash settlement. If you can find a company willing to purchase your life insurance policy for more than the cash value but less than the death benefit, this is a profitable option. The main benefit of selling permanent life insurance versus term life insurance is that a company will more than likely purchase your permanent life insurance at any stage of your life. With term life insurance, however, a company will usually only buy this policy for cash if you are likely to die during the policy term due to age or sickness.

NOTE: If you choose to sell your permanent life insurance policy for cash, you will be required to pay both income and capital gains taxes on the settlement. In addition, if you have trouble selling your life insurance on your own and decide to hire a business broker to facilitate the transaction, he or she will also be paid a portion from the settlement. That being said, selling your life insurance is usually more lucrative than surrendering your policy to the insurance company. Finding a buyer to purchase your permanent life insurance policy is not easy and could take several weeks or even months. Therefore, you may need assistance from a sales professional.

What happens once the policy is sold and you are paid? The life insurance settlement company will take over your premium payments and will become the new beneficiary of your policy.

THE BOTTOM LINE...IS CASH VALUE LIFE INSURANCE RIGHT FOR YOU?

As you can see, there are different forms of cash value life insurance and many different points to consider, making this form of permanent life insurance much more complicated than a simple term life insurance policy. You should discuss all of your options, your current financial and health situation, your beneficiaries, and any other issues with a life insurance professional and your financial adviser to see if cash value life insurance is right for your personal situation.

If you simply want to protect your family after you are gone and want simplicity with fixed premium payments that are inexpensive, term life insurance may be a better option for you. For example, young families that may not be able to afford the higher premium payments that come with permanent life insurance, but still want protection for their young children, may be better-served by a basic term life insurance plan. In addition, families that are still building their retirement accounts – 401(k)s, IRAs, etc. – may be better served allocating their funds into those accounts rather than a cash value life insurance policy. Cash value life insurance policies are more expensive than term life insurance, but there are still many circumstances in which cash value life insurances policies are the way to go:

- High-income earners with, somewhat, multifaceted finances who are more liquid and can allocate funds into the cash value portion and the death benefit portion of permanent life insurance.
- Middle-class families who would like to build cash up slowly through a whole life insurance plan, which is less expensive than the investment-type plans, while also building the death benefit for their beneficiaries.
- Individuals who may have contributed up to the limits of their retirement accounts and would like another avenue for savings that comes with interest gains based on the market, such as variable and universal life insurance policies.
- Families who are simply looking for, and can afford, another savings vehicle to be used later to cover debts, pay off insurance premiums, or complete a large purchase in the future.
- Those who have long-term savings goals may find the tax-deferred savings aspect of a cash value life insurance plan very profitable. In particular, a permanent policy plan like variable or universal life insurance would be very beneficial in this type of long-term situation.

The above bullets are just a few circumstances in which cash value life insurance could benefit an individual or family. Although these types of permanent life insurance policies are more complicated than term, they can be very useful options for saving money while you are living and protecting your loved ones when you are gone. Just remember that the premiums involved with a cash value life insurance plan can be expensive, so it is imperative that you have an understanding of how and when you should use the cash portion of your funds.

Whether you want to withdraw cash to pay off debt, take out a loan for that new pool or car, or pay off your insurance premiums, permanent life insurance can be a very beneficial, tax-free, way to save money.

One final note: if you have now decided to purchase a permanent life insurance plan, make sure you figure out what you are looking for before you decide between whole, variable, universal, or indexed life insurance. The cash you grow is tax-deferred, but will compound much differently based on the plan you choose. If you are older and do not have the applicable amount of time to grow your cash value – which may take several years – you may want to talk to a professional before looking into cash value life insurance.

MY PERSONAL EXPERIENCE

As much as I would like to stay anonymous, my personal finances drove me to write this work. I went to my financial advisor (who is also my CPA) when I thought I needed life insurance. I was young, married and had a baby on the way. My advisor explained the various options to me: term, whole life, variable, and indexed universal life. I did my fair share of research and concluded that indexed universal life was the best strategy for me. I'm so glad I made that decision! 11 years later I sit at a cash value that is much more than I put into the policy. In a few more years, I will have a paid up 1.5 million dollar policy for my family and by the time I'm 60, I will be able to pull roughly 35K a year from my policy, tax free. It's really a great thing, as I fund the policy $500 a month. This policy combined with my 401k ensures that I will truly have a great retirement (if I get social security, well that's just a bonus). I will say that these type of insurance policies can work very well, however are somewhat complex. I would absolutely recommend working with an advisor and meeting with him/her yearly.

I spoke to my financial advisor and unfortunately, he did not want to be named in this writing. However, if you're interested in learning more and want to take the next step, you can email me shanec981@gmail.com and I would be glad to make an introduction via email with him and his firm (he's in Georgia but from what he's told me, he can advise nationwide). Call me a geek, but this stuff really gets me excited!

www.ingramcontent.com/pod-product-compliance
Lightning Source LLC
Chambersburg PA
CBHW072236230526

45466CB00024B/2068